DEAR ME AT FIFTEEN

A Poetry and Self-Expression Book

By Jennae Cecelia

Dear Me At Fifteen

Interior written and designed
by Jennae Cecelia

Cover design by Islam Farid
www.islamfarid.net

ISBN: 9781730962189
This book is a work of fiction. Names,
characters, places, and incidents are
products of the author's imagination or are
used factiously. Any resemblance to actual
events of locales or personas, living or dead
is entirely coincidental.

For my readers and my dreamers-

This book is for you.
Six books in and I couldn't thank you more
for the never-ending support.
Here's to many more books, beautiful souls.

dear reader,

The poems that make up this book are bits and pieces of advice that I wish I would have known at the age of fifteen.
Being a teen is all about self-discovery, but as the years have gone on, I have realized I am constantly trying to figure out who exactly I am.

Dear Me at Fifteen is to not only inspire you to be the best version of yourself today and in the future, but for you to reflect on all the growth you have made.

As you read this book you will notice that it is half poetry and half self-expression journal.
It is meant for you to dig deep into yourself and answer questions you don't always take the time to think about.

Enjoy some inspiration and self-reflection.

ALL OF MY LOVE

♡ Jennae

I AM JUST
TRYING TO BE
THE
WOMAN
MY
fifteen-year-old
SELF WOULD HAVE
ADMIRED

YOUR MOUNTAINS
WANT YOU TO
CLIMB THEM.
NOT STAND AT
THE BASE
STARING UP AT
WHAT YOU COULD HAVE.

Write a message to the top of those mountains.
What do you think you will see at the top
when you arrive? How will that make you feel?

_____

_____

_____

_____

_____

_____

_____

_____

_____

_____

_____

_____

_____

_____

_____

_____

I TRIED TO IGNORE HER
AND PUSH HER AWAY,
BUT HER NAME WAS
ANXIETY,

AND SHE DIDN'T CARE
WHAT I ALREADY HAD
PLANNED FOR MY DAY.

When anxious thoughts appear in your mind,
what would you want to tell yourself at that
time to help you get through it?

YOUR MAP MAY
CHANGE DIRECTION
TIME AND TIME AGAIN.
BUT THAT IS WHY IT IS
CALLED A JOURNEY,
THERE IS NO
DEFINITE END.

Write about a destination on your map
you want to visit. It could be a feeling, a
place, or a person! Why do you want to
go there?

_____

_____

_____

_____

_____

_____

_____

_____

_____

_____

_____

_____

_____

_____

_____

_____

I KNOW YOU FEAR
BEING ALONE,
BUT TRUST ME
WHEN I SAY,
YOU NEED THE SPACE
TO GROW & EXPAND
AT YOUR OWN PACE.

What types of feelings do you experience when you are alone?

_____

_____

_____

_____

_____

_____

_____

_____

_____

_____

_____

_____

_____

_____

_____

you have Beauty on & Beyond your walls

Write a letter to your mind, body, and soul about how wonderful you are.

I WANT TO LET YOU KNOW THAT EVEN THOUGH YOU DIDN'T GET TO THE TOP OF THE MOUNTAIN YOU WANTED, THE ONE YOU CLIMBED INSTEAD, HAS A MUCH BETTER VIEW.

Write a letter for your future self for when things don't go as planned. Go back to read when needed.

You have so much love to give & you need to share it with yourself.

Write a letter filled with reasons why
you love yourself. Keep adding to this
list if you can't thing of many right away.

_____

_____

_____

_____

_____

_____

_____

_____

_____

_____

_____

_____

_____

_____

_____

what doesn't
make sense now
will be screaming
with certainty
in the future.

Write about a time something didn't go as planned, but turned out being one of the best things that could have happened in the situation.

_____

_____

_____

_____

_____

_____

_____

_____

_____

_____

_____

_____

_____

_____

_____

_____

REMOVE THE PEOPLE
FROM YOUR LIFE
WHO MAKE YOU FEEL
LIKE YOU CAN
HARDLY BREATHE FROM
ALL THE TOXICITY.

Make a list of all the people who bring joy
into your life and why.
If you leave out people who are involved in
your life, write about why they didn't make
your list.

the light in your eyes will NEVER go out completely. Sometimes it Needs time to Recharge.

Think of something you are super
passionate about.
What keeps you pushing towards
that passion even on days of uncertainty?

_____

_____

_____

_____

_____

_____

_____

_____

_____

_____

_____

_____

_____

_____

_____

_____

It is still a battle
everyday
to make sure
my anxious mind
doesn't apologize
for being
an anxious mind.

Write a letter to someone describing to them
something hard you battle in your daily life,
and why it is important to you that they
understand this battle.

_____

_____

_____

_____

_____

_____

_____

_____

_____

_____

_____

_____

_____

_____

_____

_____

I believe i needed
that moment in time,
when I never thought
my waves would
subside,
to show myself I was
stronger than
the tide.

What or who is your motivation to keep on
swimming forward even if the tide is rough?

Those stretch marks that you see on your hips & thighs are there because of growth and that is just fine.

Write a kind letter to your stretch marks, your zits, acne scars, or cellulite.

_____

_____

_____

_____

_____

_____

_____

_____

_____

_____

_____

_____

_____

_____

_____

_____

I JUST WANT YOU
TO KNOW,
RAIN WON'T
HIT YOUR FACE
FOREVER.
SUNRAYS ARE
COMING SOON.

What would be the first thing you would say to
the sun if it shined in your life for the first time
in awhile?

_____

_____

_____

_____

_____

_____

_____

_____

_____

_____

_____

_____

_____

_____

_____

_____

I WAS SEARCHING FOR
happiness
BUT I FOUND IT IN MYSELF.

What does happiness look like to you?
Write a letter to yourself describing your
version of what happiness is.

_____

_____

_____

_____

_____

_____

_____

_____

_____

_____

_____

_____

_____

_____

_____

_____

sometimes to find
what you want,
you have to leave
what you have.

What is something that is out of your comfort zone that you want to do?
What would it feel like to do that?
Something that both scares and excites you at the same time!

_____

_____

_____

_____

_____

_____

_____

_____

_____

_____

_____

_____

_____

_____

_____

_____

there is no

LOVE

quite like self-love

How many times a day do you tell yourself how
much you love yourself?
Why do you think it is that number?

_____

_____

_____

_____

_____

_____

_____

_____

_____

_____

_____

_____

_____

_____

_____

_____

I KNOW IT FEELS LIKE THE TIDE HAS BEEN <u>PUSHING</u> YOU OUT TO WHERE YOU DON'T WANT TO BE, BUT SOON IT WILL BEGIN TO MOVE THE WAY YOU WERE HOPING, WITH <u>EASE</u>.

Where do you want to see yourself five years from now?

_____

_____

_____

_____

_____

_____

_____

_____

_____

_____

_____

_____

_____

_____

_____

_____

they don't know
you are sad
because the smile
you know is <u>fake</u>,
they think is <u>real</u>.

What makes you smile a huge and genuine smile?

What was one of the messiest times that
you went through?
What did it teach you going forward?

I hope you realize that chasing your dreams was so worth the days of uncertainty.

If you could have one of your biggest dreams
come true, what would it be?

you are waiting
for a love
that all along
you needed from
youself.

What are small daily things you can
do to give yourself more love and care?
List them out and then start adding some
into your daily routine.

_____

_____

_____

_____

_____

_____

_____

_____

_____

_____

_____

_____

_____

_____

_____

LIFE ISN'T OUT
TO GET YOU
LIFE IS JUST
TRYING TO
TEACH YOU.

Are you happy or unhappy with your life
currently?
Why do you feel that way and what
can you do to change that?

I know my **ANXIETY** may annoy you but **IMAGINE** being the one with it.

Has anxiety ever stopped you from doing
something you wanted to do?
If so, what was it?
If you don't have anxiety,
write a letter to someone who does
and let them know you are there for them.

_____

_____

_____

_____

_____

_____

_____

_____

_____

_____

_____

_____

_____

_____

_____

OH HOW YOU WILL
BLOOM BEYOND A
SEED OR STEM.
YOU WILL BLOOM
INTO THE FLOWER
YOU ONLY COULD
SEE IN YOUR HEAD.

You are blooming into such a beautiful flower.
What flower would it be and why?
How does the flower reflect who you are?

Loving Yourself does not make you conceited. Loving Yourself is what you have always needed.

Describe yourself as if you are viewing yourself from a third-person perspective.

_____

_____

_____

_____

_____

_____

_____

_____

_____

_____

_____

_____

_____

_____

_____

_____

YOU DON'T HAVE TO PRETEND YOU ARE OKAY IF YOU ARE NOT. YOUR MENTAL HEALTH IS JUST AS CRUCIAL AS YOUR ARM HANGING OFF.

Write a letter reminding yourself just how
important your mental health is.
If you are having trouble coming up with ideas
while reading this, come back to it later when you
feel like the time is right.

_____

_____

_____

_____

_____

_____

_____

_____

_____

_____

_____

_____

_____

_____

_____

_____

happiness will wait for you, so don't worry about it leaving.

Often times we fear losing happiness.
But the truth is, happiness may come and go,
but it is never permanently gone.
Write a letter to happiness. Tell happiness
how you feel about it and how important
it is to you.

YOUR FLAWS
ARE ONLY FLAWS
IF YOU SAY
THEY ARE.

What do you consider a "flaw" on your body, and why do you view it as a flaw?

_____

_____

_____

_____

_____

_____

_____

_____

_____

_____

_____

_____

_____

_____

_____

_____

BREATHE IN.
BREATHE OUT.
DON'T LET
THOSE LUNGS FILL
WITH DOUBT.

What makes you feel doubtful? Is it a person, situation, etc.? Write a letter to the part of you that can doubt yourself at times and tell them why you don't need to be doubtful.

_____

_____

_____

_____

_____

_____

_____

_____

_____

_____

_____

_____

_____

_____

_____

_____

you may not know
who you want to be,
so take your time &
spend your days
in self-discovery.

Write a letter to who you want to be
in ten years.

_____

_____

_____

_____

_____

_____

_____

_____

_____

_____

_____

_____

_____

_____

_____

_____

there may not be
a song sung to
your liking now,
but your anthem
is releasing soon. ♪

When you anthem comes, what will it be about?

_____

_____

_____

_____

_____

_____

_____

_____

_____

_____

_____

_____

_____

_____

_____

_____

tomorrow is
the day that
you can start
living the dream
you plan on
getting to
someday.

Write out your most common daily routine.
Is that the routine you always want?
What would you like your day to day life
to look like instead, if not?

GROW AT
YOUR OWN PACE.
FLOWERS BLOOMING
SHOULD NOT
BE A RACE.

Which stage of growth are you in?
Did you just plant your seeds.
is your green stem appearing,
or is your flower in bloom?
What are you doing to continue
your growth?

This season may have unexpected weather,
but soon the forecast will look much better.

What does your perfect day look like?
This could be weather, activities, etc.
Write out your dream day!

To the people
who said I was
too quiet,
Just imagine if
you heard all
the loudness
in my head.

Describe what, "silence" sounds like
in your mind.

YOU felt like you needed an, "approach with caution" sign. With all of the activity going on in YOUR Mind.

If you could wear a shirt that said everything
you wanted people to understand about you,
what would it say?

Somedays even
doing mundane
tasks like
tying your shoe,
or brushing you hair,
can feel so
mentally exhausting
when you are
anxious or depressed.
You got this though,
lovely.
Even if your victory
is getting dressed.

What is your victory today? Big or small,
write about it!

_____

_____

_____

_____

_____

_____

_____

_____

_____

_____

_____

_____

_____

_____

_____

_____

don't forget the beauty you find in sunsets, because you know it will Rise again.

Describe what it will feel like to rise after a dark period of time.

would you be shocked
if I told you that
you are currently sitting
in a coffee shop
drinking overpriced tea,
right before you are
about to go to an event
and speak?
I am still shocked too.
All along you thought
you didn't have
a voice, and yet
here people are
listening with interest.

What is something that you have done that
still shocks you that you were able to do?
Or what is something you want to do to shock
yourself?

_____

_____

_____

_____

_____

_____

_____

_____

_____

_____

_____

_____

_____

_____

_____

_____

if you are feeling empty, let the light at the end of tunnel fill you right up.

What causes you to feel empty at times?
How do you overcome that empty feeling?

_____

_____

_____

_____

_____

_____

_____

_____

_____

_____

_____

_____

_____

_____

_____

_____

YOU CAN find out the most about yourself IN the silence you surround yourself with.

Take time to silence your mind for ten
minutes, then come back and write about
how you feel, and what is on your mind now.

I would
much rather
have the opportunity
to feel each
emotion,
even if they aren't
always great
emotions to feel.

Would you rather feel each emotion or no emotions at all? Why?

_____

_____

_____

_____

_____

_____

_____

_____

_____

_____

_____

_____

_____

_____

_____

_____

IT IS OKAY
TO DRIVE
WITHOUT A
DESTINATION
IN MIND

You have an open road ahead of you and
no worries on on your mind.
Where are you going to go and why?

_____

_____

_____

_____

_____

_____

_____

_____

_____

_____

_____

_____

_____

_____

_____

_____

you may not have all that you want Right now, but oh do you have so much greatness coming your way. Remember that on days when everything isn't going okay.

Make a list of goals you want to accomplish and how you are going to accomplish each goal.

_____

_____

_____

_____

_____

_____

_____

_____

_____

_____

_____

_____

_____

_____

_____

_____

TODAY IS GOING TO BE WHAT TOMORROW WILL CALL A BEAUTIFUL YESTERDAY.

What is something you keep saying you
will do tomorrow and why aren't you
doing it today?

THE PEOPLE YOU
THOUGHT WOULD
BE THERE TO CATCH
YOU WHEN YOU FELL,
DISAPPEARED
QUICKLY WHEN THINGS
WEREN'T GOING WELL.
DON'T BLAME YOURSELF
FOR THAT,
NOT EVERYONE CAN BE
A SAFETY NET.

Do you lean on yourself or others more
for help? Why do you think that is?

you can burn bridges, but there are pieces that still linger.

Write to someone that you burned bridges
with or haven't talked to in a long time
because of conflict.
What would you want to say to them
after all this time?

beauty comes
from the inside.
your soul, &
your mind.
it is more
than just your
hair looking
fine.

Write about what makes you beautiful
without talking about physical features.

_____

_____

_____

_____

_____

_____

_____

_____

_____

_____

_____

_____

_____

_____

_____

YOU HAVE A STORY
WITH A WHOLE
DIFFERENT PLOT.
DON'T FORGET THAT
WHEN YOU WONDER
WHY YOUR STORY
ISN'T READING
LIKE OTHER'S.

What is YOUR story?

_____

_____

_____

_____

_____

_____

_____

_____

_____

_____

_____

_____

_____

_____

_____

_____

YOU will never feel Ready enough to make life-changing decisions. that is why they are called LIFE-CHANGING

What was a life-changing decision that
you made and why was it life-changing?

_____

_____

_____

_____

_____

_____

_____

_____

_____

_____

_____

_____

_____

_____

_____

_____

As you get older
you will realize
that all along
it wasn't about
your size.
It was about
your passion,
kindness,
eagerness,
and wit.
Please don't
call it quits on
a body that is
housing so much
importance.

What do you appreciate most about
your body?

Be gentle with people
in the way that
you want people
to treat you.
It is easy to
be harsh, but
imagine the
harshness coming
at you.

Write about how you want people to treat you
and how you treat other people.

_____

_____

_____

_____

_____

_____

_____

_____

_____

_____

_____

_____

_____

_____

_____

_____

YOUR MIND IS CRAVING FOR YOU TO GIVE IT A SMALL BREAK, & RECOGNIZE ALL THE WORK THAT IT TAKES TO KEEP UP WITH WHAT MAKES YOU HAPPY.

Write about what it would feel like to
have no and plans and nothing due.
Write about how it would feel to have a
free day to do anything.

_____

_____

_____

_____

_____

_____

_____

_____

_____

_____

_____

_____

_____

_____

_____

_____

What does naturally beautiful mean to you?

LOOKING HAPPY & FEELING HAPPY SHOULD GO HAND IN HAND, & IF THEY DON'T, TAKE THE TIME TO FIND OUT WHY THAT IS.

Write about what it feels like to both look and feel happy.

_____
_____
_____
_____
_____
_____
_____
_____
_____
_____
_____
_____
_____
_____
_____
_____

YOU LOVE THE
OCEAN,
LAKE,
RIVER,
ANY BODY
OF WATER.
SO WHY AREN'T
YOU LOVING
YOUR BODY OF WATER?

What is stopping you from loving
your body 100%?

_____

_____

_____

_____

_____

_____

_____

_____

_____

_____

_____

_____

_____

_____

_____

_____

you think you are
in "love,"
but you are
really just
in "like."

What does being in love feel like to you?
This could mean being in love with
yourself or someone else.

_____

_____

_____

_____

_____

_____

_____

_____

_____

_____

_____

_____

_____

_____

_____

_____

you can be
the sunshine that
breaks through
the clouds.
you can be
that beam of
light people are
in search of.

Do you often go to others for advice or
do people come to you for advice?
Why do you think that is?

_____

_____

_____

_____

_____

_____

_____

_____

_____

_____

_____

_____

_____

_____

_____

_____

YOU HAVE THE
POWER
TO TELL A
Story
NEVER HEARD.

You have your own unique voice.
What do you want to share with people
that they can't find out from just anyone?

_____

_____

_____

_____

_____

_____

_____

_____

_____

_____

_____

_____

_____

_____

_____

_____

It is much
more fulfilling
to create something
brand new,
than copy and paste
what others do.

You have blank canvas. What are you going to paint on it?

_____

_____

_____

_____

_____

_____

_____

_____

_____

_____

_____

_____

_____

_____

_____

_____

YOU CAN'T LIVE
ONLY FOR OTHER
PEOPLE, OR JUST
YOURSELF.
IT IS ALL ABOUT
BALANCING YOUR
SELFISHNESS AND
SELFLESSNESS.

What is one selfish thing you would do
for yourself?
What is one selfless thing you would do
for someone else?

give more
compliments
give less
criticism

Do you criticize or compliment people
more and why?

It is okay
to fail while
discovering
who you are.

Have your failures stopped you from
doing what you truly wanted to do?
Why? And how can you learn from
those failures instead?

YOU HAVE SO MANY
DOORS YOU CAN
CHOOSE FROM.
OPEN THE ONE THAT
IS CALLING TO
YOU MORE.
DON'T WORRY IF
IT ISN'T THE ONE
EVERYONE ELSE
WANTED YOU TO
EXPLORE.

What is behind the door you want
to choose?

_____

_____

_____

_____

_____

_____

_____

_____

_____

_____

_____

_____

_____

_____

_____

_____

CLIMBING UP THE
mountain
IS THE
REWARDING PART.
YOU WON'T FEEL
fulfilled
GETTING DROPPED
OFF.

What was one of the most
fulfilling moments of you life thus far?

PROBLEMS WILL COME,
BUT SO WILL SOLUTIONS.
TAKE YOUR TIME TO
FIGURE OUT YOUR
RESOLUTION.

How do you handle problems?
Do you think you could handle them
better? If so, how?

YOU ARE SO WORTHY OF ALL OF YOUR DREAMS. ESPECIALLY THE ONE YOU THINK IS HARDEST TO REACH.

Do you tell yourself that you are worthy
of your biggest dream?
If not, write here why you are
worthy of it.

_____

_____

_____

_____

_____

_____

_____

_____

_____

_____

_____

_____

_____

_____

_____

_____

DRAW YOUR COMFORT zone & than move faR outside of it.

comfort zone

you

What does getting outside of your
comfort zone look and feel like to you?

_____

_____

_____

_____

_____

_____

_____

_____

_____

_____

_____

_____

_____

_____

_____

_____

What is waiting at the end of the road is worth all of these potholes.

You are almost at the end of a bumpy road. What is there when you arrive?

YOUR FLOWER MAY LOSE IT'S PETALS, BUT THAT DOESN'T MEAN IT CAN'T GROW BACK MORE.

What stage are you in right now?
Is your flower dropping more petals
than you would like?
Or is it full of petals?

_____

_____

_____

_____

_____

_____

_____

_____

_____

_____

_____

_____

_____

_____

_____

_____

Your fire may only be a few embers left behind, but you can always add more wood to spark a bigger light.

What lights the fire inside of you?
What do you do when that light
starts to dim?

give today
the chance to
prove it won't
be like your
terrible
yesterday.

If today was a bad day, what would you
normally do when having a bad day?
Is there a better way you can handle
your bad days?

Sometimes life may feel like there is only time to go in a drive-thru line. But you will get your time to sit down & enjoy a three course meal without worrying about the pace of your life.

What do you consider being busy?
Are you busy because you have a lot to do
or are you busy because you aren't
managing your time in the best way?

IF YOU ONLY STAY
ON THE SAME PATH,
YOUR SCENERY WILL
GET BORING AND
REPETITIVE.

How long have you been on your
current path in life?
Are you happy with the scenery?
Why or why not?

YOU CAN BE
AS GREAT AS YOU
HOPE TO BE.
YOU JUST HAVE
TO HAVE THE
RIGHT MENTALITY.

Remind yourself once an hour today
that, "you are great."
Then come back at the end of the day
and write how you feel here.

wait for the person who makes your stomach & mind flutter with excitement. The one who loves you equally.

Do the people you surround yourself with
make you feel 100% happy with who
you are with them?
Why or why not?

you can ask
everyone for
advice, but
sometimes only
you know what
is best for your
mind, body, & soul.

Leave yourself a piece of advice here to
come back to when you need it.

_____

_____

_____

_____

_____

_____

_____

_____

_____

_____

_____

_____

_____

_____

_____

_____

YOU CAN BE
KIND
WITHOUT
LETTING
PEOPLE
WALK ALL
OVER YOUR
MIND

Write about how it is ok to say, "no"
and not feel one bit bad about it.

_____

_____

_____

_____

_____

_____

_____

_____

_____

_____

_____

_____

_____

_____

_____

_____

WHEN YOU ALLOW
YOURSELF TO RISE,
OH WILL YOU BLOOM.

What fears do you have about succeeding?
Whether it is in a career or relationships,
why do you fear it?

If people don't believe your truth that says more about them than you.

Spill your truth onto this page.
Maybe it is something no one knows
about you, or maybe it is something
no one believes is true.

YOU HAVE SO MANY POSSIBILITIES KNOCKING AT YOUR DOOR THAT YOU SHOULD NOT IGNORE.

What opportunity have you been ignoring
but should be paying more attention to?

_____

_____

_____

_____

_____

_____

_____

_____

_____

_____

_____

_____

_____

_____

_____

_____

YOU CAN
LIGHT
YOUR OWN
CANDLE

Write a letter the ten-year-old
you, and tell them what you would
have wanted to hear then.

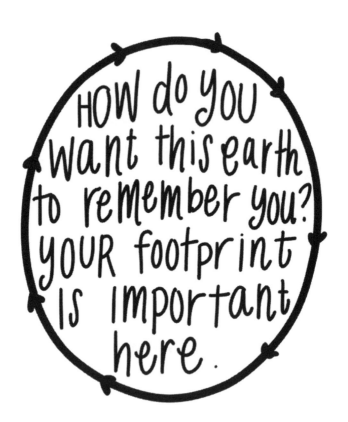

How do you want this earth to
remember you?

The people in
your life will
change like the
seasons.
And each will
come with their
own weather.
You don't have to
let their forecast
become yours.

What does your forecast look like today
and why?

_____

_____

_____

_____

_____

_____

_____

_____

_____

_____

_____

_____

_____

_____

_____

_____

HOLD THAT EXCITEMENT
YOU FEEL ON THE FIRST
MORNING OF SUMMER
TIGHT WITH YOU THROUGH
LIFE.

Imagine that it is the first day of summer
and you have no worries at all.
What type of day would you want?

Carry an open mind with you through all the doors that close.

Are you open minded or close minded
and why?

SOMETIMES WRITING
OUT YOUR FEELINGS
IS MORE POWERFUL
THAN SPEAKING THEM.
WE TEND TO HOLD BACK
LESS WITH JUST A
PEN & PAPER AS THE
RECIPIENT.

Do you prefer to write out your feelings
or talk them out, and why?

_____

_____

_____

_____

_____

_____

_____

_____

_____

_____

_____

_____

_____

_____

_____

YOU HAVE the `POWER` to paint YOUR walls a `COLOR` that embodies positive emotions.

What color are you going to paint your
walls and why?

Someone is
in need of
the message
inside of
your soul.

What are a few pieces of advice you have
that you feel like others would benefit
from knowing.
Write them here and then share with
a friend who may need to hear what you
have to say.

THE EARTH
MAY SHAKE
TO WAKE YOU
UP. IT WANTS
YOU TO REMEMBER
EVEN THOUGH
THIS FEELS TOUGH
YOU HAVE THE
STRENGTH TO RISE
ABOVE.

Write a letter to yourself to wake you
up when you are doubting your
strength to rise.

YOU ARE MORE THAN
A BODY,
YOU ARE SOUL
FILLED WITH PURPOSE.

Write a letter to your soul.

You are a tree with strong roots and full branches standing tall through the winds.

What type of tree do you think represents
you best and why?

_____

_____

_____

_____

_____

_____

_____

_____

_____

_____

_____

_____

_____

_____

_____

YOU DON'T NEED
A LOVER TO EXPERIENCE
LOVE.

Do you invest more time into
finding love from yourself or
finding love with someone else?
Why?

enjoy each stage
you enter because
one day you will
look back & miss
what once didn't
seem important.

Write about a time in your life when something didn't seem important at the time, but now you miss it.

_____

_____

_____

_____

_____

_____

_____

_____

_____

_____

_____

_____

_____

_____

_____

DON'T WASTE
YOUR HARD EARNED
MONEY TRYING
TO IMPRESS
ALL OF THE
PEOPLE CONSIDERED
WELL DRESSED.

Do you dress to impress other people
or do you do it for yourself?
Why?

Travel around
in your mind
with the same
curiosity you
would travel
the world
with.

Are you more curious about how
your mind works or the world works?
Why?

_____

_____

_____

_____

_____

_____

_____

_____

_____

_____

_____

_____

_____

_____

_____

_____

YOU MAY FIND FRIENDS
IN HIGH QUANTITIES,
BUT NOT ALWAYS
IN HIGH QUALITY.

Do you prefer to have a lot of friends
or a few quality friends?
Why?

YOU will make it through these **MURKY** times, and find the opportunity to **RISE**, like a lotus from the **mud**.

Remember that time you thought that this was the worst thing that could happen to you, how did you overcome that?

_____

_____

_____

_____

_____

_____

_____

_____

_____

_____

_____

_____

_____

_____

_____

YOU ARE WAITING
TO HEAR FROM
the universe,
BUT THE UNIVERSE
IS WAITING TO
HEAR FROM YOU.

Write a message to the Universe, God,
or any higher power you believe in.
If you don't believe in anything, then
write a letter to yourself with all the
things you are hoping for in life right now.

Cherish the moments
you have with
the people you love.
Because one day
you will miss the
view, the smells,
and the laughter
you can't replicate.

If you could replicate any moment
in time, what would it be?

my self-care list

 meditate

 - read

 go out for coffee

 buy flowers

 go on a hike

 write

Draw your self-care list here

Calming My ANXIETY

 DRAWING    JOURNAL

 MEDITATION   ♪ MUSIC

 SHUTTING OFF ELECTRONICS

Draw what you do to calm your anxiety. If you don't have anxiety, draw what calms you.

Breath in, breath out.
I hope you are left feeling inspired
and filled with less doubt.
Thank you!

Acknowledgements

Thank you to every single one of you
who is constantly supporting my writing.
My gratitude and happiness grows more
and more each day.

To my love, my friends, and my family,
I thank you so much for encouraging
me to chase my dreams.

To the fifteen-year-old me, I hope
you can see how much you have grown,
and these are all things I wish you could
have known.

About the Author

Jennae Cecelia is a best-selling author of inspirational poetry books, and is best known for her book, *Uncaged Wallflower*.

She is also an inspirational speaker who digs into topics like self-love, self-care, mental health, and body positivity.

Her mission is to encourage people to reach their full potential and live a life filled with positivity and love.

jennae cecelia

JennaeCecelia@gmail.com

Social Media: @JennaeCecelia

Read More of Jennae's books

Bright Minds Empty Souls
Uncaged Wallflower
I Am More Than a Daydream
Uncaged Wallflower-Extended
I Am More Than My Nightmares

All Available on Amazon.com

Printed in Great Britain
by Amazon